George Parada • **Robert Wróblewski** • **Mike Koenig** • **Stefan Dramiński**

HETZER & G-13

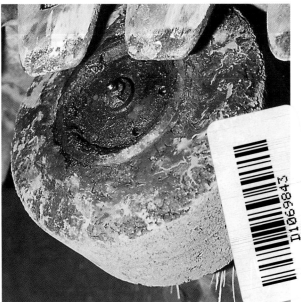

KAGERO

In March 1943, Col. Gen. Heinz Guderian demanded a light tank destroyer to replace all existing „interim solutions" (e.g. Marders) and towed anti-tank artillery (e.g. 75mm PaK 40 guns). The result of this was the Panzerjägerprogram. The new vehicle resulting from it was to equip tank destroyer units of infantry divisions. The Panzerkampfwagen 38(t) chassis was chosen as a base for this new Panzerjäger. It was first known as "Leichtes Sturmgeschutz 38(t)", then "Jagdpanzer 38(t) für 7.5cm Pak 39 L/48", and finally "Jagdpanzer 38 Hetzer". It appears that the name Hetzer was not an official name but used by troops and then used in postwar publications. On December 17, 1943, designs were ready and, on January 24, 1944, a wooden mock-up was finished. In March 1944, the first three prototypes were produced by BMM (Boehmish-Mährische Maschinenfabrik) and it was decided to start production. From March to April of 1944, prototypes were extensively tested, while preparations for production were made at BMM (Praga/CKD—Ceskomoravska Kolben Danek) in Prague and then at Skoda Works at Pilsen.

On April 20, 1944, the Hetzer was shown to Hitler and other leaders of the Third Reich at Arys (Orzysz) in East Prussia. At this time, the new Panzerjäger was designated Jagdpanzer 38(t) Hetzer (Baiter or Troublemaker), Sd.Kfz.138/2, but it was also known simply as Panzerjäger 38(t). Production started, in April 1944, at BMM and, in September, at Skoda. 2,584 were produced by May 1945 in three series (chassis numbers 321001-323000 by BMM, 323001-unknown by Skoda, and 325001-unknown). In April 1944, BMM produced the first 20 Hetzers and monthly production increased greatly thereafter. Eventually, plants in Prague, Pilsen, Königgrätz, Boehm, and Breslau made the Hetzer. Late-war production plans called for 1,000 Hetzers per month, starting in mid-1945.

The Hetzer was built on the Panzerkampfwagen 38(t)'s widened chassis with modified suspension (larger road-wheels from the Praga TNH n.A prototype reconnaissance tank) and an upgraded engine. The new engine was the 160hp Praga AC/2 6-cylinder engine controlled by a Praga-Wilson gearbox (5 forward and 1 reverse gears). The chassis was modified to accommodate a larger gun and thicker armor than was used with the regular PzKpfw 38(t). The Hetzer carried 320 liters (84 US gallons) of fuel in two tanks, which gave it maximum range of 177 km (110 miles). Its combat weight was 16 metric tons (17.6 short tons) and it could travel at a maximum speed of some 42km/h (26 mph). The Hetzer's tracks had 96 links per side, were 350mm wide and had a surface contact of 2.72m (8.8 feet).

The Hetzer had a low, well-sloped hull of welded construction. The hull had a 60mm-thick frontal plate, 8mm roof armor and 20mm side and rear armor. All armored plates sloped inward. In addition, the Hetzer was fitted with small 5mm-thick side skirts (Schürzen) to protect the hull and upper track run from shaped charges, as were used in the American bazooka, for instance. It was armed with a 75mm PaK 39 L/48 gun with limited traverse (5 degrees to the left and 11 degrees to the right) and elevation (-6 degrees to +10 degrees). It was equipped with a Sfl.Z.F.1a gun sight. The main armament was protected by a 60mm cast gun mantlet, which was dubbed "Saukopf", or "pig's head" because of its shape. The heavy gun and thick frontal plate overloaded the vehicle at the front, but this problem was later corrected by strengthening the suspension.

The main gun had an effective range of over 1,000 meters (1,083 yards). For example, the Hetzer could knock out a Soviet T-34/85 at a distance of 700 m (760 yards) with a hit on the frontal armor, while the T-34/85 could kill a Hetzer at a distance of 400 m (433 yards)

Jagdpanzer 38 "Hetzer", early production version. Vehicle captured by American army. *(Icks collection, Patton Museum Library)*

Jagdpanzer 38 "Hetzer", early production version. Vehicle has untypical mazzle brake. *(Icks collection, Patton Museum Library)*

with a frontal hit. In comparison with a JS-2, the Hetzer could be knocked out at a distance of 1,000m, while the Hetzer had to be within 100m (108 yards) to kill a JS-2. The limited traverse of the gun forced Hetzer crews to change vehicle position constantly to shift to other targets, thus exposing the thin 20mm side armor to enemy fire. An interesting feature was the remotely controlled MG34/42 mounted on the roof, with 360 degrees rotation for local defense. The machine gun had a 50-round drum magazine and could be aimed and fired from inside the vehicle. However, the loader was then exposed to enemy fire for reloading. The late StuG III also used this machine gun system.

The Hetzer's interior was cramped for the four-man crew (commander, gunner, loader and driver), because of its sloped armor and low silhouette. The interior was divided into two compartments—engine and fighting/crew compartment. The gunner and loader were located on the left side of the gun, and the driver sat in front of them, while the commander was in the rear, on the right side of the gun. The crew communicated using an intercom system and a 10-watt FuG5 radio set. Hetzers completed as command vehicles—Befehlswagen 38(t) Hetzer—had an additional 30-watt FuG8 radio set.

The commander could observe the battlefield using periscopic binoculars through an open hatch in the roof, but, overall, his field of view was very limited, especially to the left front, and the driver often had to determine how to position the vehicle to shoot. The low silhouette made it difficult to spot and, at the same time, often gave the Hetzer an advantage of attacking first. The 75 mm anti-tank gun was mounted 380 mm right of center. This created difficulties for the crew, especially the gunner and loader, since the weapon itself was designed to be loaded from the right, resulting in a low rate of fire. The small interior space allowed stowage of only 40-41 rounds of 75 mm ammunition, along with 600 rounds of 7.92mm ammunition for the MG34. Storage space was later increased slightly to 45 rounds of 75 mm ammunition.

The Hetzer was constantly modified and detailed during production, and there are numerous differences among early-, mid– and late-production vehicles. Most of the changes simplified production and reflected shortages of materials. These included: modified commander's and access hatches, a lighter gun mantlet (30mm thick), modified road wheels, various types of idlers, strengthened suspension and a different muffler.

The main training center for Hetzer crews was the Panzerjägerschule at Milovice, Czechoslovakia. Hetzers were used to equip tank destroyer units (Panzerjäger Abteilungen/Panzerjäger Kompanien) of infantry divisions, panzergrenadier divisions and independent units. The majority were issued to Wehrmacht infantry divisions (starting in July of 1944) with the 15th and 76th Infantry Divisions and Volksgrenadier divisions. Hetzers were also issued as replacements to other units for Marders and other Jagdpanzers.

In the last months of the war, Hetzers were often issued as replacements for lost battle tanks, a role for which they were not intended (e.g. Panzer Divisions Kurmark and Feldherrnhalle). Some were issued to improvised units that were created in the last days of the war from various military personnel. The Hetzer was also one of the last German armored fighting vehicles that remained in production and was issued to the troops until the last days of the war.

Hetzers equipped all types of formations of the Wehrmacht, Waffen-SS (10 divisions), Luftwaffe (1 division), Kriegsmarine (2 divisions), RAD (3 divisions) and ROA (Russian Liberation Army) and saw service on all fronts. Large number of Hetzers took part in the German offensive in the Ardennes in late 1944.

Hetzers first entered service with the 731st and 743rd Heeres Panzerjäger Abteilungen in May/June of 1944. Each unit received 45 Hetzers and saw service on the Eastern Front. Following this, Hetzers were issued to three more independent units—the 741st (1944), 561st (1945) and 744th Heeres Panzerjäger Abteilungen (1945).

Jagdpanzer 38(t) "Hetzer". Vehicle was produced in November 1944. Production number: **321 111.** *(Icks collection, Patton Museum Library)*

The Waffen-SS received some 200 Hetzers, which were mainly issued to Panzergrenadier units. The first unit so equipped was the 8th SS Cavalry Division Florian Geyer in September 1944.

In December 1944, 20 Hetzers were converted into flamethrowers for the upcoming Ardennes Offensive. A flame projector, the 14mm Flammenwerfer 41, was fitted in the standard barrel to camouflage its real role as a flamethrower. All were attached to the 352nd and 353rd Panzer-Flamm-Kompanien assigned to Army Group G during the Ardennes Offensive.

In early 1945, a few Hetzers were rearmed with the Panther's 75mm KwK 42 L/70 to increase firepower. After tests, this idea was rejected since the long-barreled gun made the nose extremely heavy and the entire vehicle less mobile and more difficult to operate.

Designers planned to use the Hetzer chassis and hull for several other purposes, such as a flakpanzer, but none of them reached production stage. In November 1944, the Jagdpanzer 38(t) was chosen as a base for the 150mm sIG33/2 howitzer. From December 1944 to the end of the war, thirty carriers were produced by BMM (Praga/CKD). They were designated as 15cm Schweres Infanteriegeschuetz 33/2 (Sf) auf Jagdpanzer 38(t)

Hetzer. From October 1944, 106 Bergepanzer 38(t) Hetzer were produced, including with 64 Hetzers converted to this light recovery purpose.

To simplify production, development started, in December 1943 on the Jagdpanzer 38(t) Hetzer Starr, armed with a recoilless 75mm PaK 39/1 L/48 in a rigid mount. An assault gun variant, armed with the 105mm StuH 42/2 L/28 gun, was also intended as part of the E-Series, to be based on the PzKpfw 38(d) chassis. Eventually, the Jagdpanzer 38(d), based on the PzKpfw 38(d) and armed with either a 75mm PaK 39 L/48 or a 75mm PzJagK 42 L/70, was to replace the Hetzer. The end of the war terminated the entire 38(d) project, also part of the E-Series. In November 1944, it was also decided to utilize the Hetzer chassis as a base for a Flakpanzer 38(t) Hetzer (Kleiner Kugelblitz) mounted with the turret (possibly with different armament) designed for the Flakpanzer IV Kugelblitz, but it never materialized due to the war situation. Krupp made an interesting proposal to mount a PzKpfw IV turret on the Hetzer, but it did not work. Krupp also proposed to mount on the Hetzer a modified PzKpfw IV turret armed with the 80mm PAW (Panzerabwehrwerfer) 600, a smoothbore anti-tank gun. This, too, was dropped for lack of time and materials.

Jagdpanzer 38 "Hetzer". Vehicle produced in Skoda plant, "ambush" camouflage. *(Icks collection, Patton Museum Library)*

Jagdpanzer 38 „Hetzer". The same vehicle after returning from combat unit to production plant for repair. *(Icks collection, Patton Museum Library)*

In the summer of 1944, Germany planned to deliver 30 Hetzers to the Romanian Army but, instead, they were sent to the Wehrmacht. From October/November of 1944 to January/February of 1945, Germany exported 75 to 100 Hetzers to Hungary, the only other official user of Hetzers during the war. A few captured Hetzers were briefly used by Polish, American, Soviet and Bulgarian units. Probably the most notable Hetzer (from the 743rd Panzerjaeger Abteilung) was that captured by the Polish Home Army during the Warsaw Uprising on August 2, 1944. It was repaired and nicknamed „Chwat" (Gallant/Brave Fellow) and was used against its previous owners.

After May 1945, production of the Hetzer, now designated ST (Stihac Tanku)-I, continued at Skoda and Praga Works in Czechoslovakia until the early 1960s. These facilities also repaired abandoned and damaged vehicles. The Czechoslovakian Army was equipped with some 249 ST-1 vehicles in 1949 and used them until the mid/late 1950s. The Swedish army probably used Hetzers after the war until the early 1960s. The Swiss army purchased some 158 Hetzers between 1946 and 1952. These remained in service, designated as G-13, until the early 1970s. The G-13 was armed with a 75mm StuK 40 gun as planned by German designers during the war. The Swiss made various modifications to the G-13 to modernize it (e.g. some were fitted with 6-cylinder, 150hp diesel engines and were designated G-13D). Also, Israel was interested in purchasing 65 ST-Is, but, because of their high price (twice that of a Sherman), the transaction was abandoned. A small numbers of Hetzers remained in use by Warsaw Pact armies into the 1950s.

The Jagdpanzer 38(t) Hetzer was cheap, fast, low and hard-hitting. It is considered to be one of the most successful tank destroyers of World War II. It was not popular with crews, for the cramped space and poor external vision made it difficult to use. It proved to be a dangerous opponent on the defensive, however, and it was one of the best German tank-hunters of the late war period. The Hetzer's design is still considered to be a base for some modern tank destroyers, most notably the Swedish Stridsvagn 103 (S-Tank).

Today, Hetzer and its variants can be seen on display in many locations. These include: a Hetzer at Axvall, Sweden; a G-13 modified to Hetzer standards at Panzermuseum Munster, Germany; an unarmed Hetzer and a post-war ST-1 at Lesany, Czech Republic; a Hetzer at the Imperial War Museum in Duxford, England; a Hetzer in the Museum of the Polish Army in Warsaw, Poland; a Hetzer NIIBT at Kubinka, Russia; a G-13 modified to Hetzer standards at Bastogne Historical Center, Belgium; a Hetzer at Bovington Tank Museum, England; a Hetzer at Worthington Park Museum, Canada; a G-13 at the National Museum of Military History in Diekirch, Luxembourg; a Hetzer and a G-13 at the Swiss Army Panzermuseum in Thun, Switzerland; a G-13 at the Auto & Technik Museum in Sinsheim, Germany; a G-13 converted to Hetzer standards at the Royal Army Museum in Brussels, Belgium; a G-13 modified to Hetzer standards at the Texas Military Forces Museum, USA; and a Hetzer at US Army Ordnance Museum, Aberdeen Proving Grounds, Maryland, USA.

George Parada

Hetzer & G-13 • **George Parada, Robert Wróblewski, Mike Koenig, Stefan Dramiński**
First edition • LUBLIN 2007 • ISBN 978-83-60445-76-1

© Wszystkie prawa zastrzeżone. All rights reserved. Wykorzystywanie fragmentów tej książki do przedruków w gazetach i czasopismach, w audycjach radiowych i programach telewizyjnych bez pisemnej zgody Wydawcy jest zabronione. Nazwa serii zastrzeżona.
Redakcja: **Stanisław Jabłoński** • Tłumaczenie: **Tomasz Szlagor** • Rysunek na pierwszej stronie okładki: **Arkadiusz Wróbel.**
Plansze barwne: **Stefan Dramiński** • Rysunki techniczne: **Stefan Dramiński** • Design: **KAGERO STUDIO**

Oficyna Wydawnicza KAGERO • www.kagero.pl • e-mail: kagero@kagero.pl, marketing@kagero.pl

Redakcja, Marketing, Dystrybucja: OW KAGERO, ul. Mełgiewska 7-9, 20-952 Lublin
tel.: (+48) 081 749 20 20, tel./fax (+48) 081 749 11 81, 0609 543 927, 0601 401 157, www.kagero.pl

Jagdpanzer 38 "Hetzer" early production version at plant yard. *(Icks collection, Patton Museum Library)*

Jagdpanzer 38 "Hetzer" early production version. *(Icks collection, Patton Museum Library)*

Jagdpanzer 38 "Hetzer" – "Merry Blade" – captured by Warsaw insurgents on August 2nd, 1944.

Jagdpanzer 38 "Hetzer" armed with 14 mm Flammenwerfer 41 flame-thrower. Vehicle captured by American army in Ardens. *(Icks collection, Patton Museum Library)*

Jagdpanzer 38 "Hetzer" produced by Skoda plant. Western front, 1944.

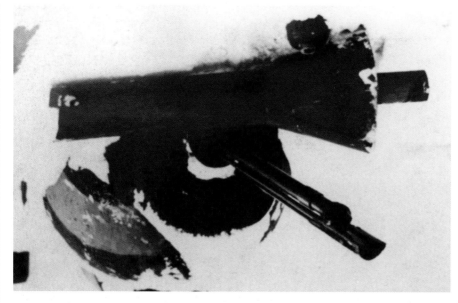

Flammenwerfer 41 flame-thrower mounted instead of a gun. *(Icks collection, Patton Museum Library)*

Jagdpanzer 38 "Hetzer" armed with 14 mm Flammenwerfer 41 flame-thrower. Vehicle captured by American army in Ardens. *(Icks collection, Patton Museum Library)*

Hetzer – Renate Boss – knocked out in Danzig (presently Gdańsk) area in March 1945.

Hetzer coded "153" (previously "003"), Prague, May 1945. • Hetzer numer 153 poprzednio 003 w Pradze w maju 1945 roku.

Hetzer coded "211" destroyed in Bohemia (presently Czech Republic) in 1945. • Hetzer numer 211 zniszczony w Czechach w 1945 roku.

Hetzer coded "T-033" destroyed by its own crew in Hungary in 1945. • Hetzer numer T-033 zniszczony przez własną załogę na Węgrzech w 1945 roku.

Hetzer abandoned in Bohemia in May 1945. • Hetzer porzucony w Czechach w maju 1945 roku.

Hetzer Steffi, Bohemia, May 1945. • Hetzer Steffi w Czechach w maju 1945 roku.

Hetzer coded "T-038" captured by Russian troops in Hungary in 1945. • Hetzer T-038 zdobyty przez wojska radzieckie na Węgrzech w 1945 roku.

Hetzer Marika coded "T-040", knocked out in Hungary in 1945. • Hetzer T-040 Marika zniszczony na Węgrzech w 1945 roku.

Hetzer in factory finish, destroyed in February 1945 in Budapest area. • Hetzer w fabrycznym kamuflażu zniszczony w lutym 1945 roku w rejonie Budapesztu.

Hetzer of 320. Panzer-Division, destroyed in 1945 in Ostrava area. • Hetzer z 320 DP zniszczony w 1945 roku w rejonie Ostrawy.

Hetzer destroyed during street fighting in Prague in May 1945. • Hetzer zniszczony na ulicach Pragi w maju 1945 roku.

Hetzer knocked out by American M 10 tank destroyer in November 1944 in Halloville, France. • Hetzer zniszczony przez amerykański M 10 w listopadzie 1944 roku w Halloville we Francji.

Hetzer destroyed in Berlin in April 1945. • Hetzer zniszczony w Berlinie w kwietniu 1945 roku.

Hetzer destroyed in February 1945 in Budapest area. • Hetzer zniszczony w lutym 1945 roku w rejonie Budapesztu.

Another Hetzer destroyed in February 1945 in Budapest area. Number 115 was painted by Russians counting their war booty • Hetzer zniszczony w lutym 1945 w rejonie Budapesztu. Numer 115 jest oznaczeniem radzieckiej zdobyczy wojennej.

Hetzer destroyed in May 1945 west of Berlin. • Hetzer zniszczony w maju 1945 roku na zachód od Berlina.

Hetzer destroyed in March 1945 in Gdańsk area. • Hetzer zniszczony w marcu 1945 roku w rejonie Gdańska.

Hetzer of 2nd Company, Pz.Jg.Abt. 743, captured by the Polish Insurgentson 2nd August 1944 at the corner of Boudena and Szpitalna streets in Warsaw. • Hetzer z 2 kompanii 743 dppanc zdobyty przez Powstańców Warszawskich 2 sierpnia 1944 roku na rogu ulicy Boduena i Szpitalnej w Warszawie.

The same vehicle in the Polish Insurgent Army's markings. • Ten sam Hetzer już w oznaczeniu powstańczym.

Two shots of restored G-13, which external details are almost the same as in original Hetzer had. The vehicle is owned by 2nd Armored Productions from Clarksville, Indiana, USA. • Dwa ujęcia odrestaurowanego G-13, który szczegółami ze-wnętrznymi niemal nie różni się od oryginalnego Hetzera. Eksponat stanowi własność 2. Armored Productions z Clarksvil-e, Indiana, USA. (Mike Koenig 2003, also credit 2nd Armored Productions, Clarksville, Indiana, USA)

One more shot of Clarksville exhibit. This vehicle is not thrown open to public. • Jeszcze jedno ujęcie eksponatu z Clark-sville. Ten egzemplarz nie jest jeszcze udostępniony zwiedzającym. *(Mike Koenig 2001)*

Right side of G-13, rear part. Visible is external equipment. • Prawy bok G-13 , część tylna. Dobrze widoczne wyposażenie zewnętrzne. *(Mike Koenig 2001)*

Close view of the driver's twin periscope protected by steel hood. • Zbliżenie na podwójny peryskop kierowcy osłonięty stalowym daszkiem. *(Mike Koenig 2003)*

Gun yoke top view. Visible are joinings of armored plates. • Jarzmo armaty widziane od góry. Dobrze widoczne łączenia płyt pancernych. *(Mike Koenig 2003, also credit 2nd Armored Productions)*

Guide bar and movable gun periscope cover.   •   Prowadnica i ruchoma pokrywa peryskopu działa. *(Mike Koenig 2003, also credit 2nd Armored Productions)*

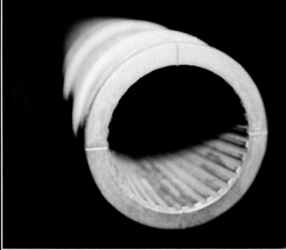

Rifled end of barrel main gun Stuk 40, 75 mm caliber. Original Hetzer had Pak 39 L/48, 75 mm cal gun.   •   Gwintowana końcówka lufy armaty Stuk 40 kalibru 75 mm. W oryginalnym Hetzerze montowano działo Pak 39 L/48 kalibru 75 mm. *(Mike Koenig 2003)*

Saukopf type gun yoke seen from the right. Wooden jack base on the foreground.   •   Jarzmo armaty typu Saukopf widziane z prawej strony. Na pierwszym planie drewniana podstawa podnośnika. *(Mike Koenig 2003)*

Numbering and lettering of the vehicle are not original, they were painted at 2nd Armored Productions. Note welded and interlocked arrmor plates. • Numery i nazwa pojazdu nie są oryginalne, zostały namalowane w 2 Armored Productions. Na zdjęciu dobrze widoczne łączenie zachodzących na siebie płyt. *(Mike Koenig 2003)*

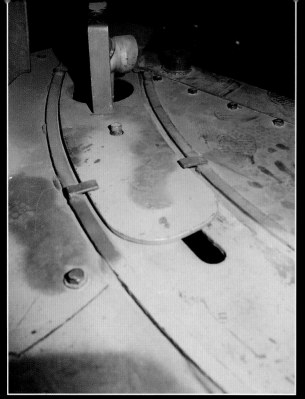

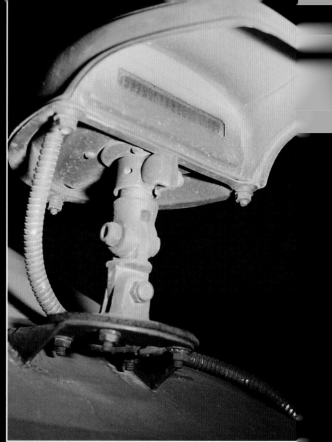

Next shot of cover and periscope. Note shield of periscope glass. • Kolejne ujęcie przedstawiające pokrywę i peryskop. Zwraca uwagę osłona szkła peryskopu. *(Mike Koenig 2003)*

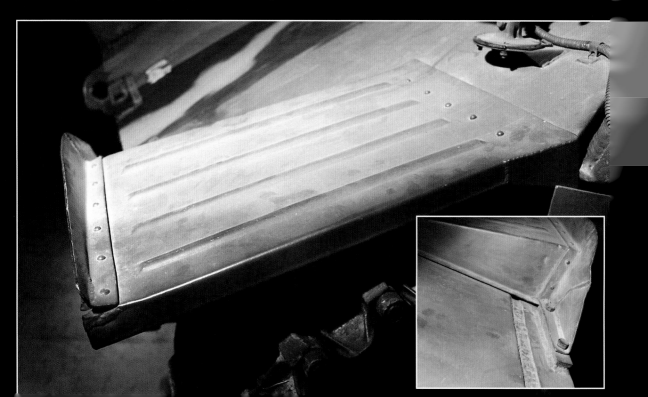

Mount of remote controlled MG 34 in open position (upper and and lower left photo) and shield of drive wheel on the right side of vehicle with visible oil valve. • Sterowany z wnętrza pojazdu uchwyt karabinu maszynowego MG 34 w pozycji otwartej (górne i dolne lewe zdjęcie) oraz osłona koła napędowego po prawej stronie pojazdu z widocznym zaworem olejowym. *(Mike Koenig 2003, also credit 2nd Armored Productions)*

Side plate with mounts of side shields of driving system. • Boczna płyta pojazdu z uchwytami bocznych osłon układu jezdnego. *(Mike Koenig 2003)*

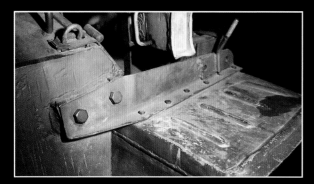

Rear left fender with bracket and jack. Track adjustment fitting. Toolbox of the rear part of left fender. • Tylni, prawy błotnik z widocznym wspornikiem i podnośnikiem. Mechanizm napinania gąsienicy. Skrzynka z narzędziami na końcu lewego błotnika. *(Mike Koenig 2003)*

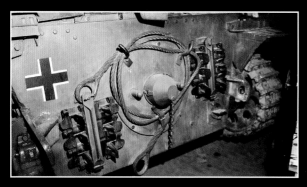
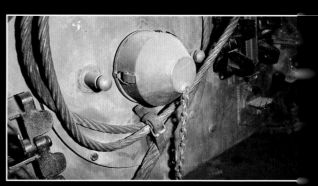

Rear view of bottom engine plate with towing cable, spare tracks and convoy light. Early type lamp not being mounted in Hetzers. Note starting crank shield. • Tylnia, dolna płyta silnikowa z liną holowniczą, dodatkowymi ogniwami gąsienicy i lampą konwojową. Lampa wczesnego typu, nie występująca w Hetzerach. Zwraca uwagę osłona wejścia na korbę do

Radio holder and 75 mm ammo fastening on left side of crew compartment. • Uchwyt na radio i mocowania amunicji 75 mm z lewej strony przedziału bojowego. *(Mike Koenig 2003, also credit 2nd Armored Productions)*

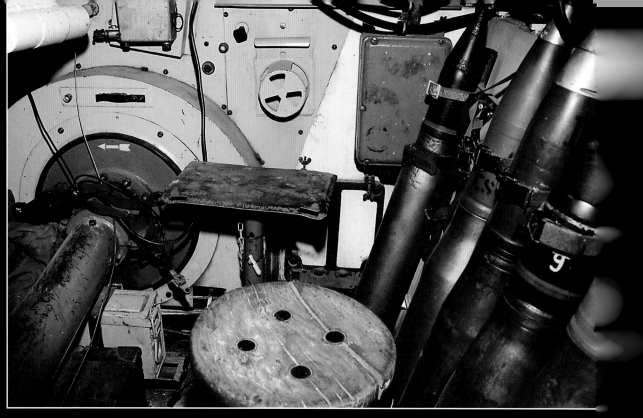

Rear view of crew compartment with visible gunner's and loeader's seats. Driving shaft with visible container for MG 34 ammo. • Widok na tył przedziału bojowego z widocznymi siedzeniami działonowego i ładowniczego. Wał napędowy z widocznym zasobnikiem na amunicję do MG 34. *(Mike Koenig 2003)*

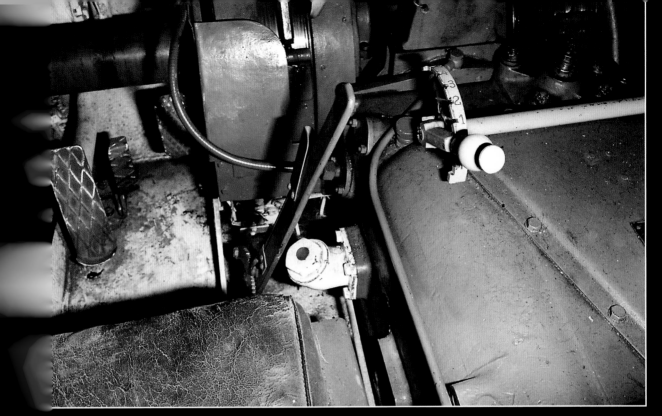

Brake mechanism on left side of vehicle and two shots of driver's position. • Mechanizm hamulcowy po lewej stronie pojazdu, mocowanie przekładni bocznej oraz dwa ujęcia stanowiska kierowcy. *(Mike Koenig 2003, also credit 2nd Armored Productions)*

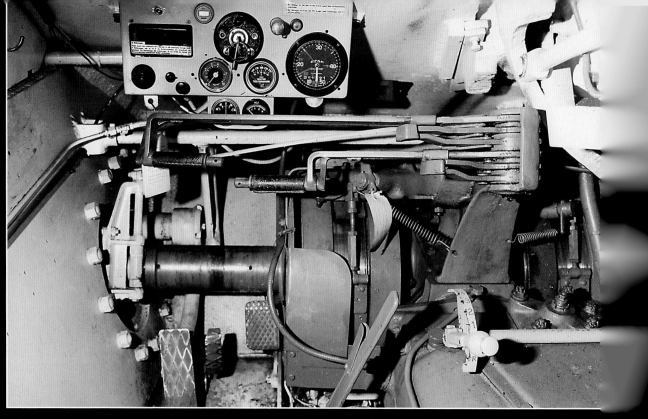

Driver's position and close view of instrument panel and twin periscopes. • Stanowisko kierowcy oraz zbliżenie na desk
rozdzielcza i dwa podwójne peryskopy. *(Mike Koenig 2003)*

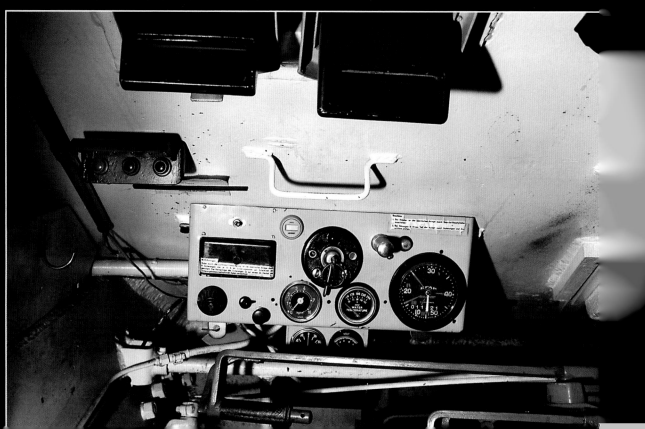

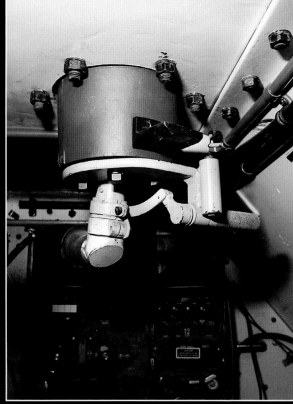

Interior of crew compartment with visible periscope mounted near MG controlled from interior. • Wnętrze przedziału bojowego z widocznym peryskopem zamontowanym obok sterowanego z wnętrza karabinu maszynowego. *(Mike Koenig 2003)*

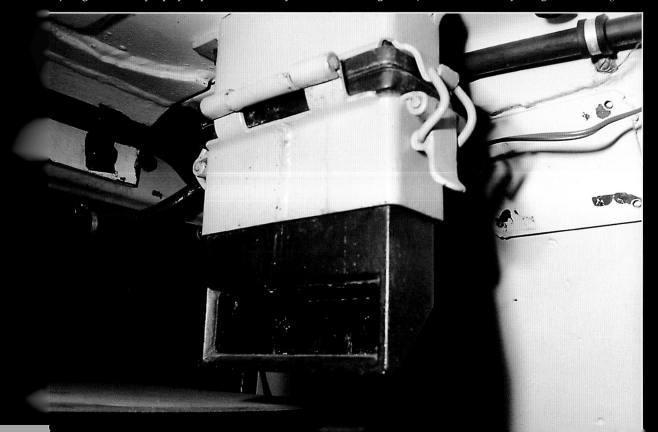

Elements of driving system on this and next pages. • Na tej i następnej stronie elementy układu jezdnego pojazdu. *(Mike Koenig 2003)*

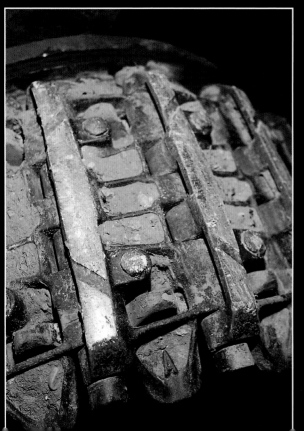

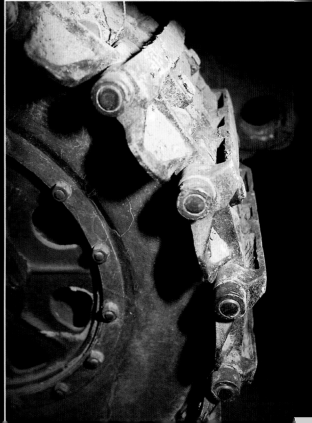

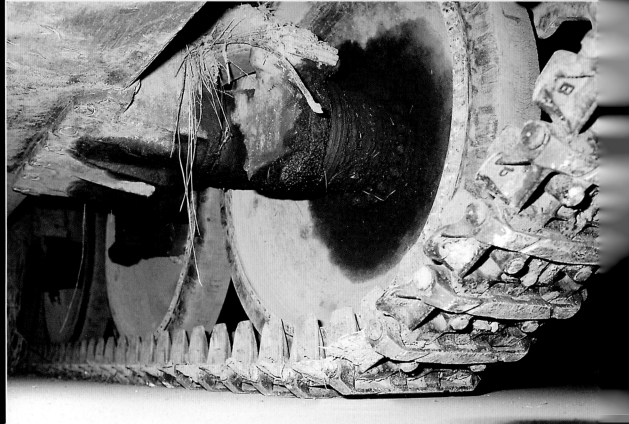

Jack mounted on right side, on the rear fender. • Podnośnik montowany po prawej stronie, na tylnym błotniku. *(Mike Koenig 2003)*

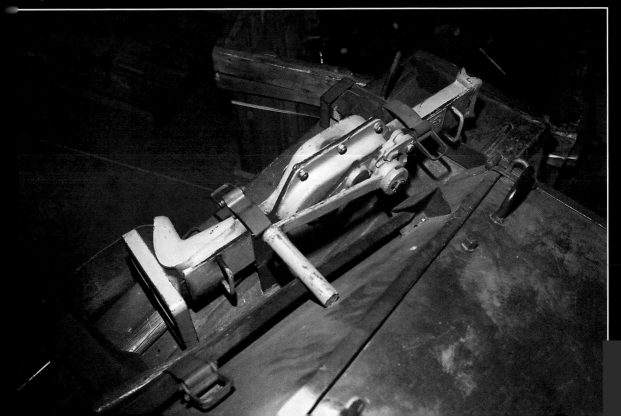

Cover of gine air intake, periscope near gunner's left hutch, lamp, gunner's hatch with lock and tool (not sure if it is original part). • Pokrywa wylotu powietrza chłodzącego silnik, peryskop obok lewego włazu ładowniczego, lampka marszowa, właz ładowniczego z zamkiem i narzędziem (nie wiadomo czy widoczne na zdjęciu narzędzie jest oryginalne)
(Mike Koenig 2003, also credit 2nd Armored Productions)

G-13 adapted to Hetzer at Patton Museum of Cavalry and Armor store. • **G-13 stylizowany na Hetzera w magazynie Patton Museum of Cavarly and Amor.** *(Mike Koenig 2003, also credit Patton Museum of Cavalry & Armor)*

Visible is rear right fender with jack, rear left fender with toolbox, upper armor plate with open commander's and loader's hatches. • Dobrze widoczny tylny, prawy błotnik z podnośnikiem, tylni lewy błotnik ze skrzynką narzędziową, górna płyta pancerna pojazdu z otwartymi włazami dowódcy i ładowniczego. *(Mike Koenig 2003, also credit Patton Museum of Cavalry & Armor)*

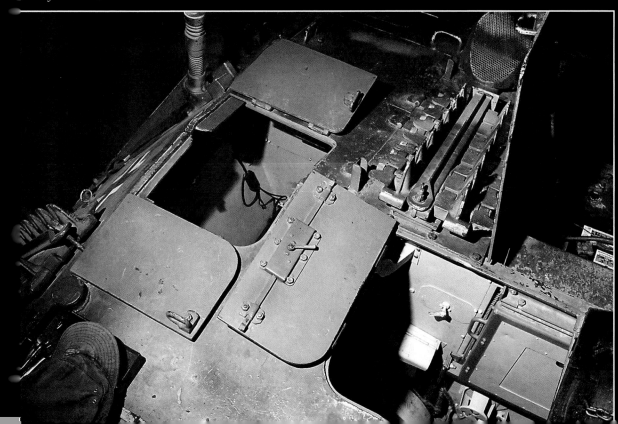

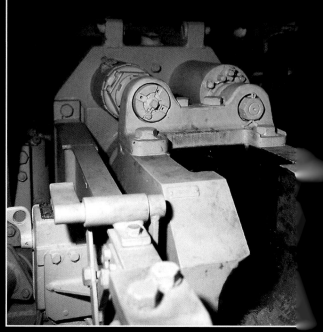

Gun Stuk 40 left view from engine compartment. Note lock on vehicle roof. • Działo Stuk 40 widziane od tyłu z przedziału silnikowego. Zwraca uwagę zamek marszowy na dachu pojazdu. *(Mike Koenig 2003, also credit Patton Museum of Cavalry & Armor)*

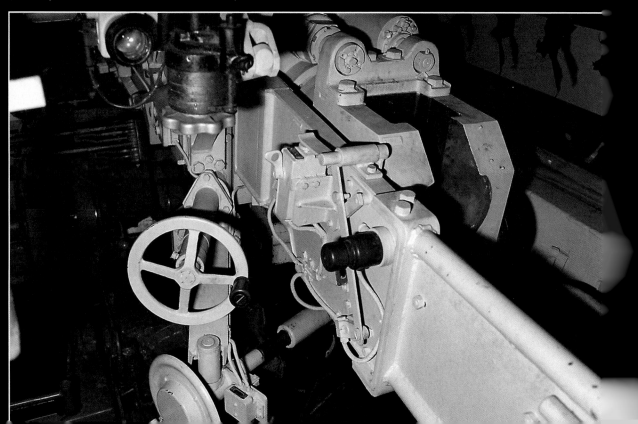

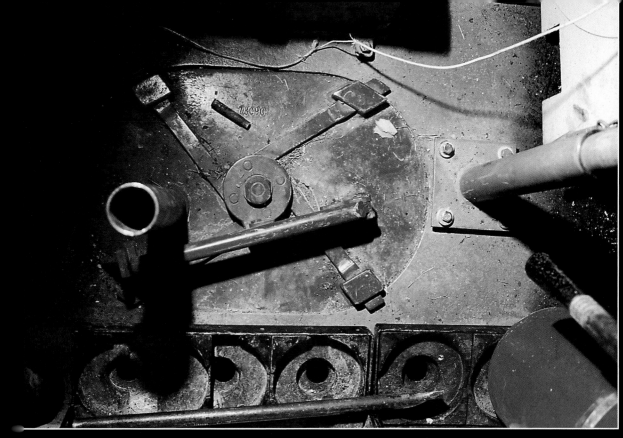

Emergency hatch in combat compartment floor. Gun visible from driver's position, control box on rear plate of fighting compartment. • Właz ewakuacyjny w podłodze przedziału bojowego. Widok na działo ze stanowiska kierowcy, skrzynka kontrolna na tylnej płycie przedziału bojowego. *(Mike Koenig 2003, also credit Patton Museum of Cavalry & Armor)*

Gunsight of Sfl.Z.F.1a gun visible from the interior and outside the vehicle. • Celownik działa Sfl.Z.F.1a widziany od środka i na zewnątrz pojazdu. *(Mike Koenig 2003, also credit Patton Museum of Cavalry & Armor)*

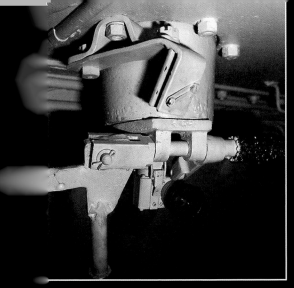

Mechanism with MG gunsight controlled from inside vehicle, driving system brake levers, steering lever and istrument panel above, front ammo holders with visible gun bracket. • Mechanizm wraz z celownikiem karabinu maszynowego kierowanego z wnętrza pojazdu, dzwignie hamulców systemu kierowania pojazdu, dźwignie kierowania i nad nimi deska rozdzielcza, przednie uchwyty na amunicję z widocznym wspornikiem działa. (Mike Koenig 2003, also credit Patton Museum of Cavalry & Armor)

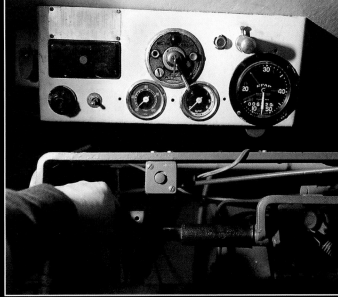

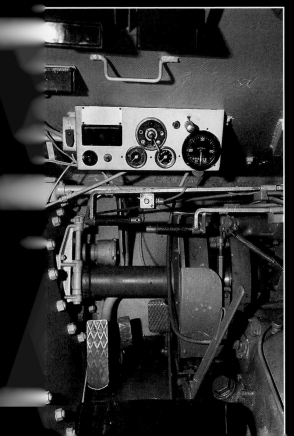

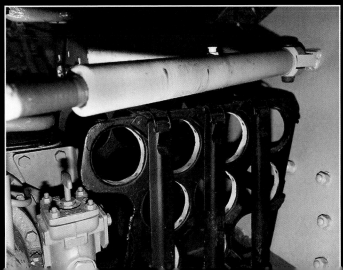

Engine view. Near dismounted cooler. • Widok silnika. Z boku wymontowana chłodnica. (Mike Koenig 2003, also credi
Patton Museum)

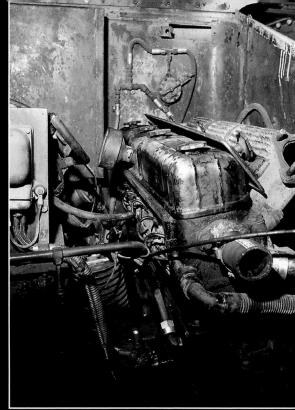

Engine compartment as seen from rear. Twin air filters mounted on right side of engine compartment. • Przedział silni-
kowy widziany od tyłu. Podwójne filtry powietrza zamontowane po prawej stronie przedziału silnikowego. *(Mike Koenig
2003, also credit Patton Museum of Cavalry & Armor)*

Elements of engine rear plate with seat for cold starting and dismounted seat for cold starting during maintenance. • Elementy tylnej płyty silnikowej z gniazdem do awaryjnego rozruchu oraz wymontowane gniazdo do zimnego rozruchu w trakcie konserwacji. *(Mike Koenig 2003, also credit Patton Museum)*

Fully reconditioned radiator awaiting reinstallation in the Patton Hetzer. • **Odnowiona chłodnica, przygotowana do zamotowania w Hetzerze.** *(Mike Koenig 2003, also credit Patton Museum)*

A few photos of external details. Note cover of exhaust pipe, holder of spare drive wheel, Notek on left front side of vehicle and a lamp i metal housing made by workshop in Swizterland. • Kilka zdjęć detali charakterystycznych dla G-13. Zwraca uwagę osłona rury wydechowej, uchwyt na jezdne koło zapasowe, Notek po lewej, przedniej stronie pojazdu oraz lampa w metalowej osłonie wykonana przez warsztaty w Szwajcarii. *(Mike Koenig 2003, also credit Patton Museum Collection)*

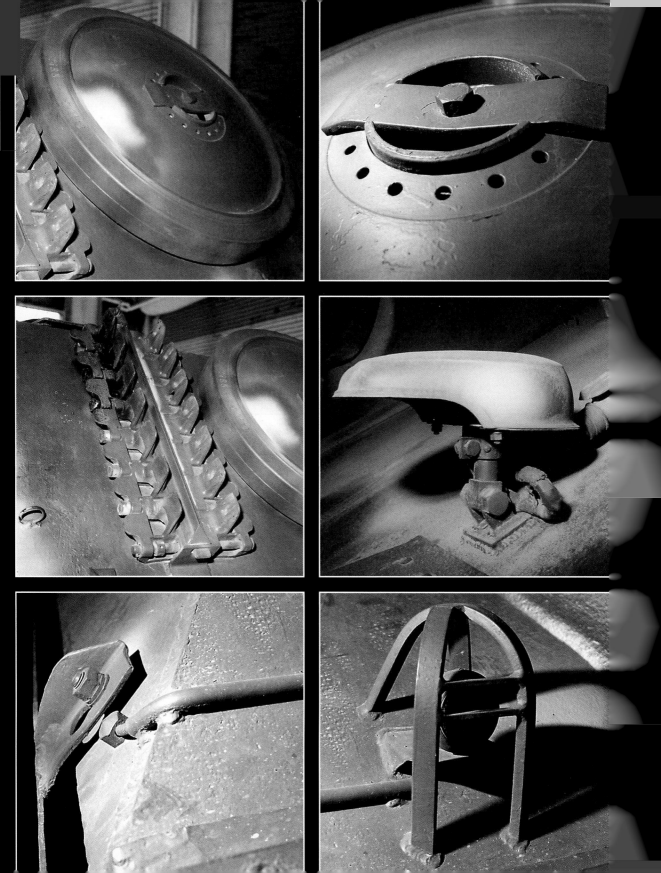

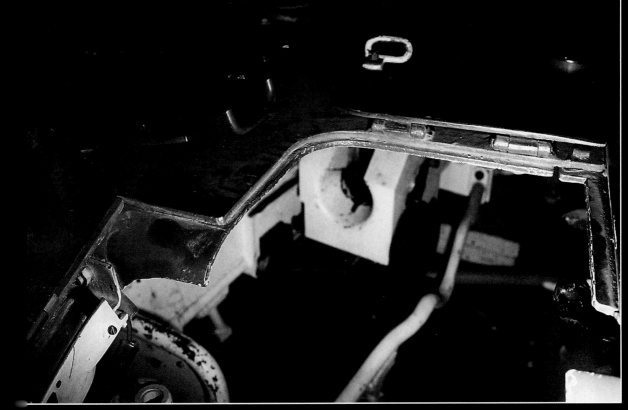

Gun as seen through commander's hatch. View on rear wall of fighting compartment with American radio equipment. •
Widok na działo przez właz dowódcy. Widok na tylnią ścianę przedziału bojowego z amerykańskim wyposażeniem radio-
wym. *(Mike Koenig 2003, also credit 2nd Armored Productions)*

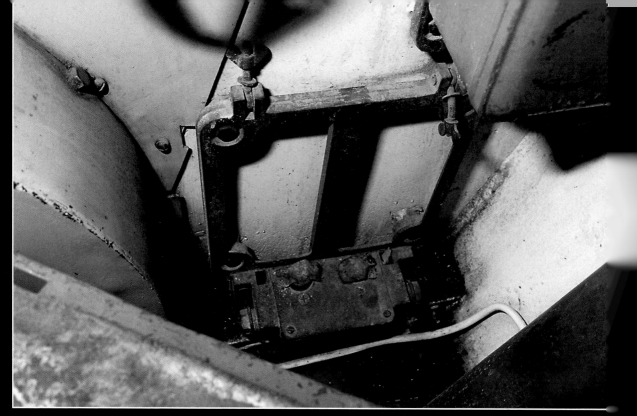

Radio mounting frame, ammo holders near commander's position, control panel with a cover mounted on rear wall of fighting compartment. • Rama montażowa zasilacza radiostacji, uchwyty na amunicję koło stanowiska dowódcy, panel kontrolny z pokrywą zamontowaną na tylnej ścianie przedziału bojowego. *(Mike Koenig 2003, also credit 2nd Armored Productions)*

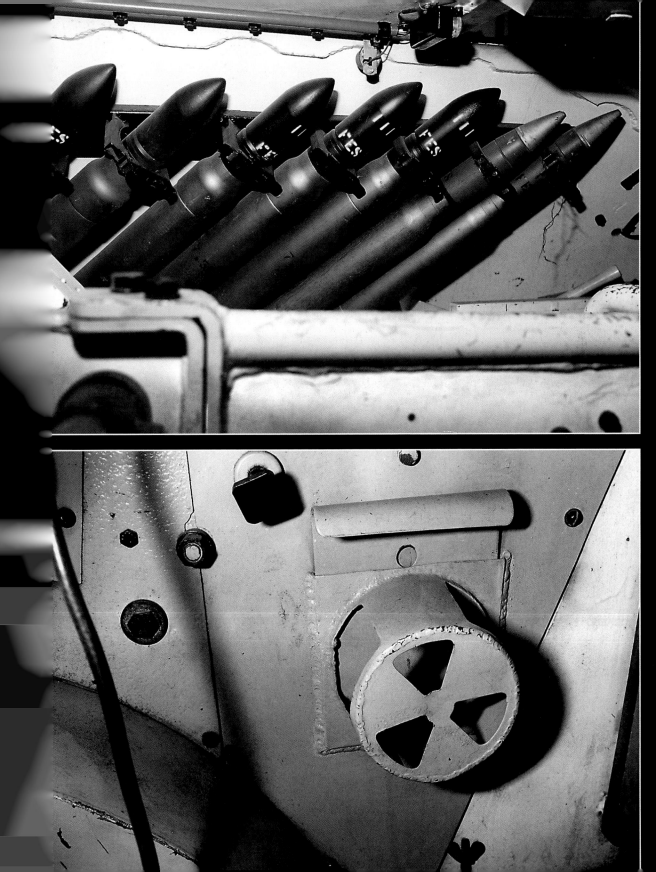

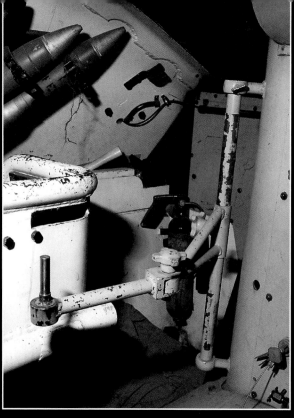

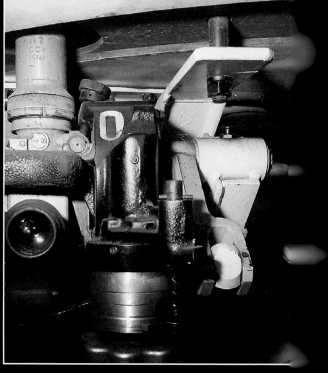

Base of commander folding scissors glass. Gun optical instruments, gunner's periscope, indicator of gun height in yoke. • Podstawa składanej lornety nożycowej dowódcy pojazdu. Przyrządy optyczne działa, peryskop działonowego, wskaźnik wysokości działa w jarzmie. *(Mike Koenig 2003 also credit 2nd Armored Productions)*

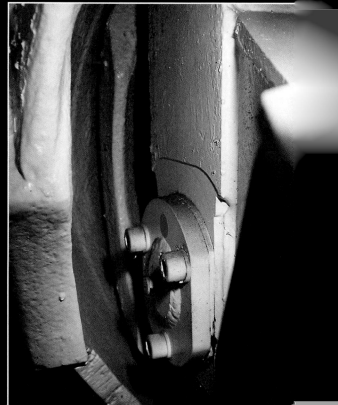

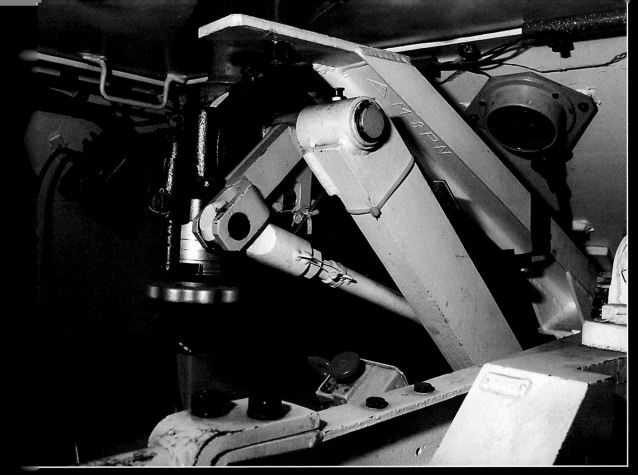

Gunner's position. • Stanowisko działonowego. (Mike Koenig 2003, also credit 2nd Armored Productions)

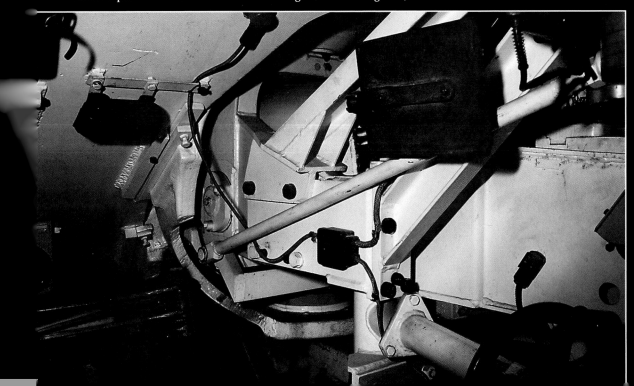

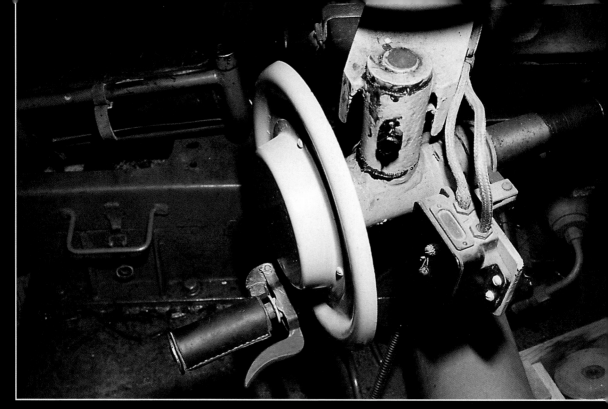

Interior of fighting compartment with visible handwheels of lifting gear and gun breech. • Wnętrze przedziału bojowego z widocznymi pokrętłami mechanizmu podniesieniowego i zamkiem działa. *(Mike Koenig 2003, also credit 2nd Armored Productions)*

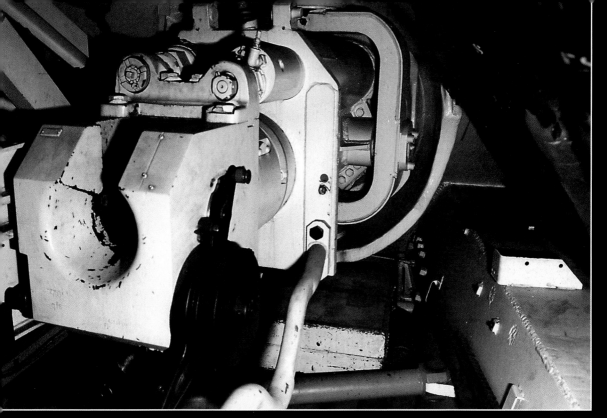

Right side of gunlock and close up of gun breech. • Prawa strona zamku działa oraz zbliżenie na zamek działa. *(Mike Koenig 2003)*

Right side of gun shield and uderside of gun breech in open position. • Prawa strona działa z tarczą ochronną oraz dó
zamka działa z klinem w pozycji otwartej. *(Mike Koenig 2003, also credit 2nd Armored Productions)*

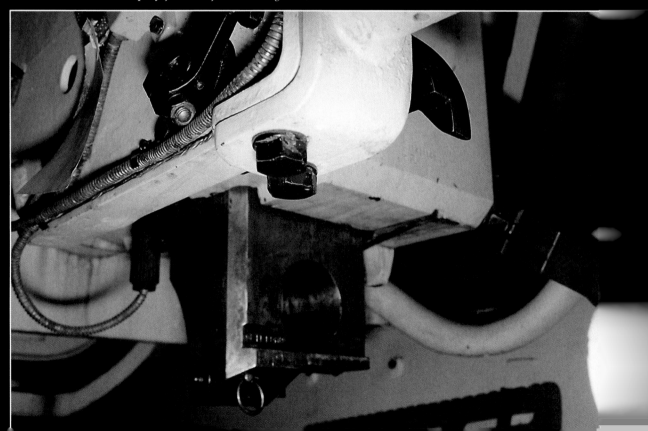

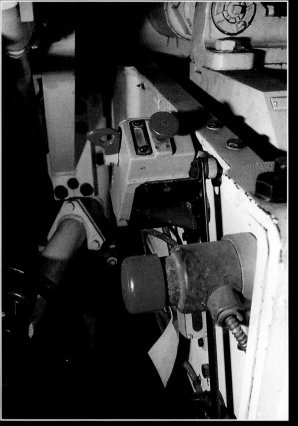

Electric system of gun firing and bottom part of yoke. • **Elektryczny system odpalania działa oraz spód jarzma.** *(Mike Koenig 2003)*

Front ammo storage with gun bracket, engine air intake, top center of crew compartment, gun with visible breech on roof of vehicle, gun yoke welded to to upper plate of crew compartment. • Przedni zasobnik na amunicję ze wspornikiem działa, wlot powietrza do silnika na środku tylnej ściany przedziału bojowego, działo z widocznym zamkiem marszowym na dachu pojazdu, jarzmo działa przyspawane do górnej płyty przedziału bojowego. *(Mike Koenig 2003, also credit 2nd Armored Productions)*

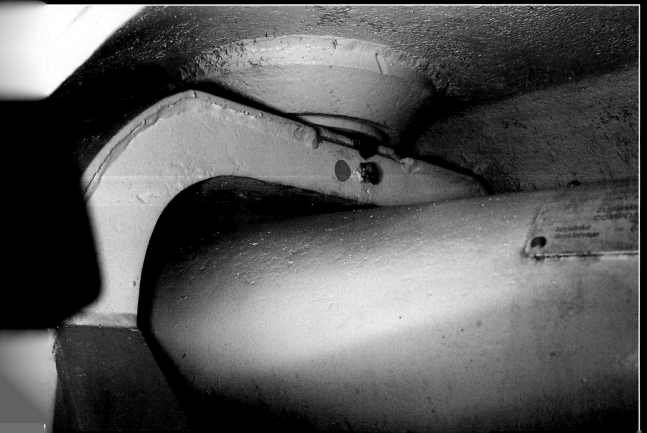

Part of floor with mount for 75 mm shells on left side of crew compartment. First aid kit on right from driver's position mounted on drive shaft housing. Wooden seat of gunner, ammo storage and escape hatch. • Fragment podłogi z podstawą na pociski 75 mm z lewej strony przedziału bojowego. Zestaw pierwszej pomocy na prawo od stanowiska kierowcy na obudowie wału napędowego. Właz ewakuacyjny, drewniane siedzenie działonowego, uchwyt na amunicję i właz ratunkowy. *(Mike Koenig 2003, also credit 2nd Armored Productions)*

Original Hetzer from Aberdeen Museum. • Oryginalny Hetzer znajdujący się w zbiorach muzeum w Aberdeen. (Krzysz

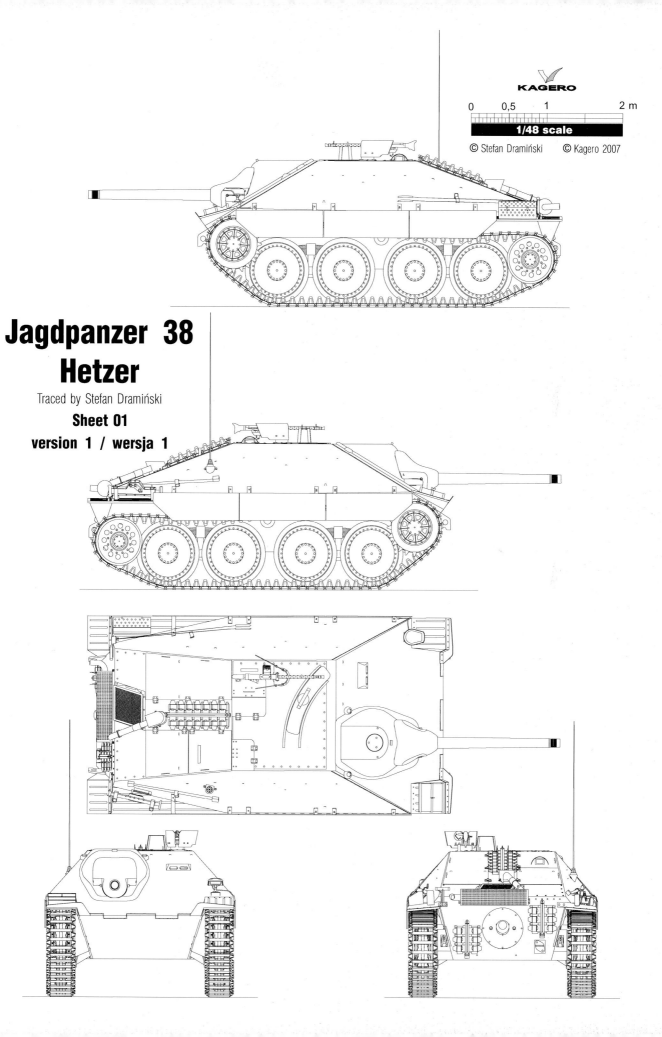

Jagdpanzer 38
Hetzer

Traced by Stefan Dramiński

Sheet 01
version 1 / wersja 1

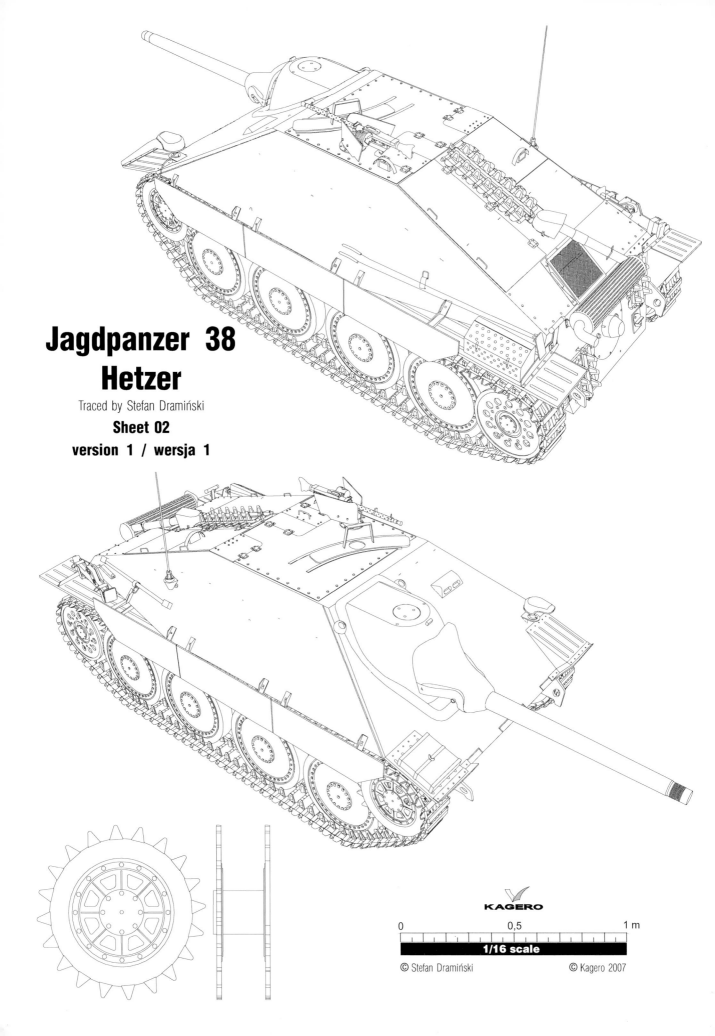

Jagdpanzer 38
Hetzer

Traced by Stefan Dramiński

Sheet 02

version 1 / wersja 1

KAGERO

0   0,5   1 m

1/16 scale

© Stefan Dramiński   © Kagero 2007

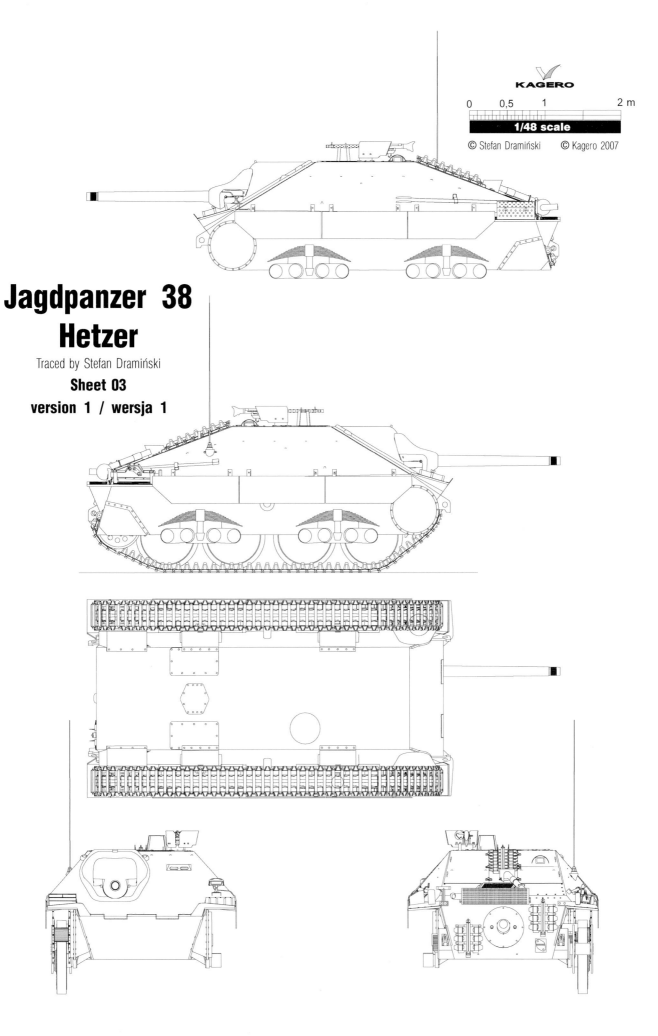

Jagdpanzer 38
Hetzer

Traced by Stefan Dramiński

Sheet 03

version 1 / wersja 1

0   0,5   1   2 m

1/48 scale

© Stefan Dramiński   © Kagero 2007

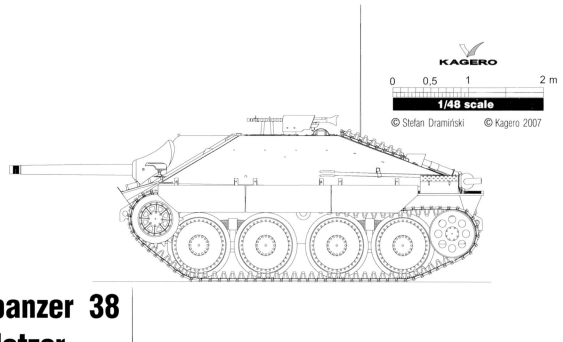

0   0,5   1   2 m
1/48 scale

Jagdpanzer 38
Hetzer

Traced by Stefan Dramiński

Sheet 04

version 2 / wersja 2

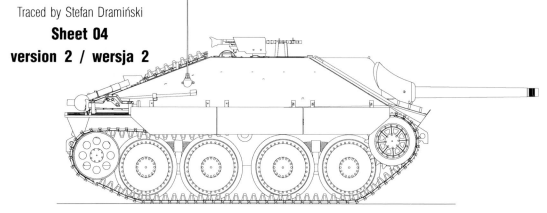

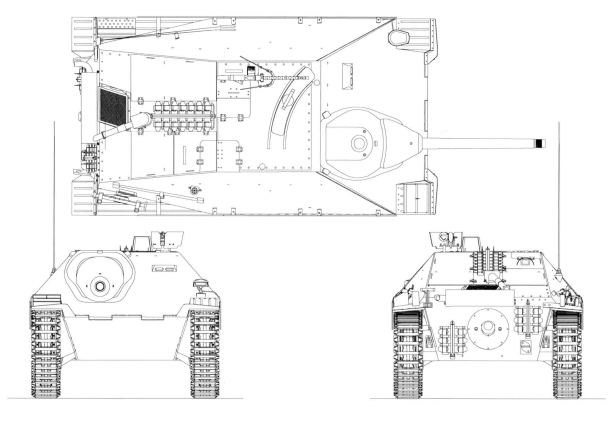

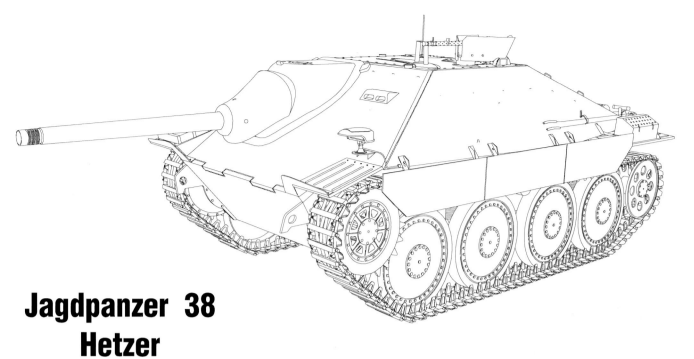

Jagdpanzer 38
Hetzer

Traced by Stefan Dramiński

Sheet 05

version 2 / wersja 2

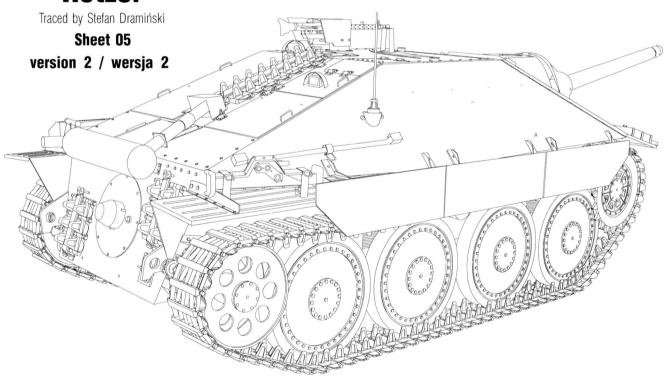

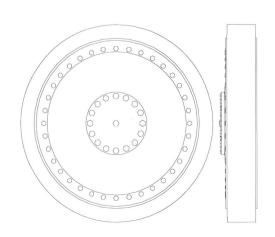

KAGERO

0   0,5   1 m

1/16 scale

© Stefan Dramiński   © Kagero 2007

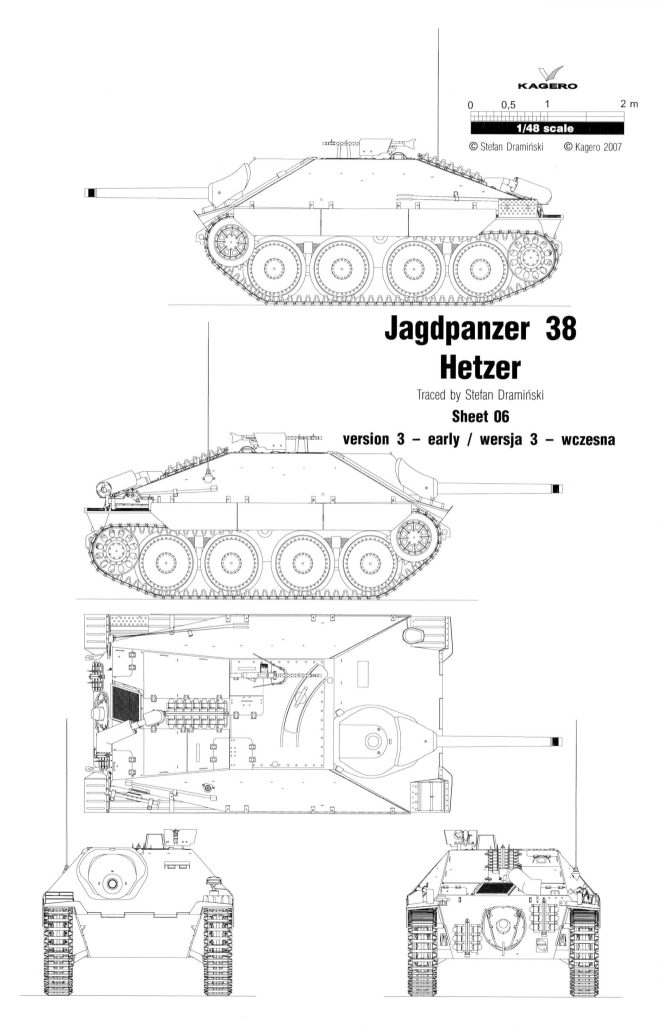

0   0,5   1   2 m
1/48 scale

Jagdpanzer 38
Hetzer

Traced by Stefan Dramiński

Sheet 06

version 3 – early / wersja 3 – wczesna

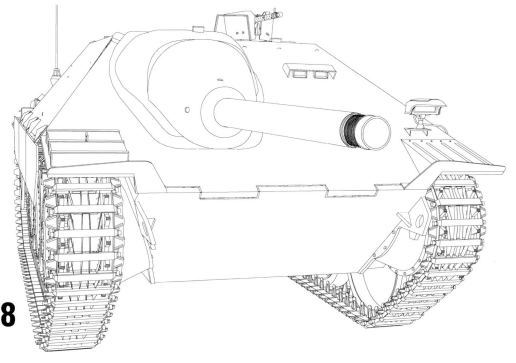

Jagdpanzer 38 Hetzer

Traced by Stefan Dramiński

Sheet 07

**version 3 - early /
wersja 3 - wczesna**

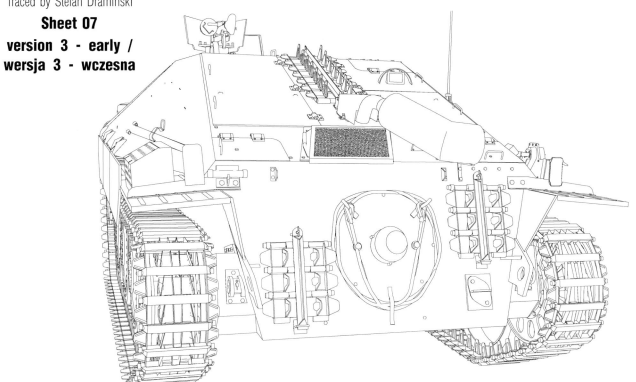

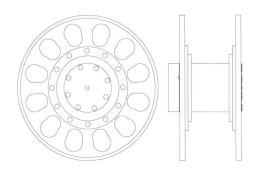

KAGERO

0   0,5   1 m

1/16 scale

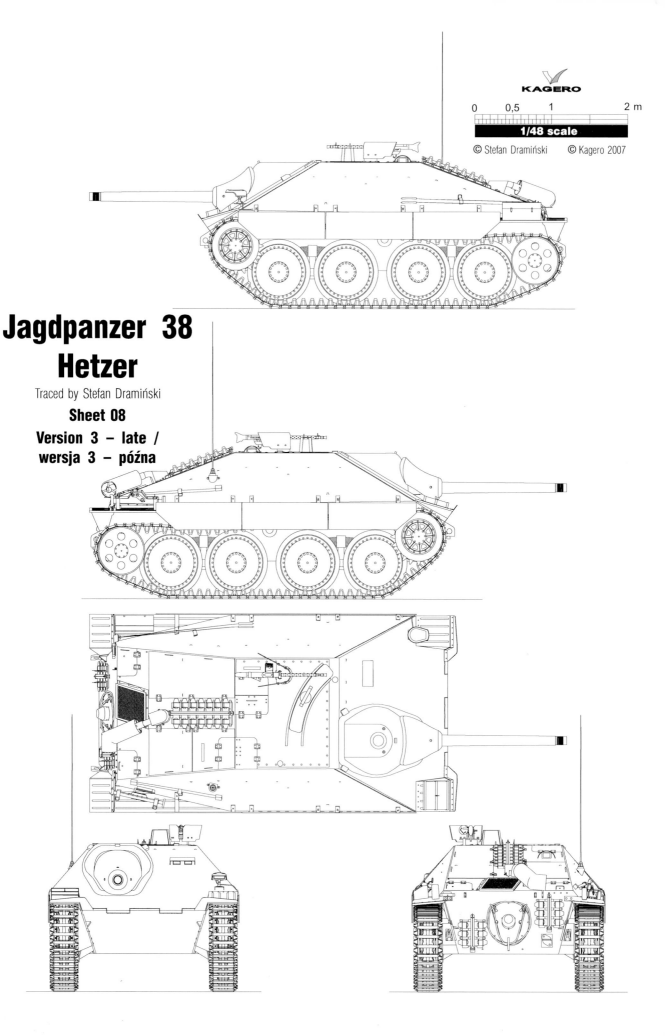

Jagdpanzer 38
Hetzer

Traced by Stefan Dramiński

Sheet 08

Version 3 – late /
wersja 3 – późna

KAGERO

0   0,5   1   2 m

1/48 scale

© Stefan Dramiński   © Kagero 2007

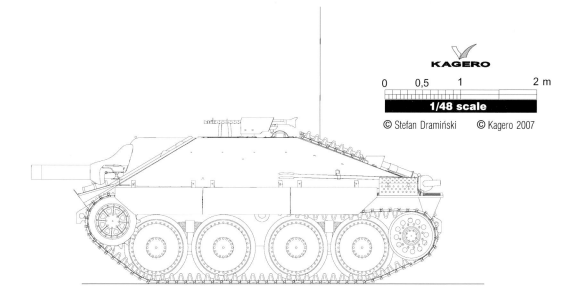

KAGERO

0   0,5   1   2 m

1/48 scale

© Stefan Dramiński   © Kagero 2007

StuH 42/2 auf
Jagdpanzer 38

Traced by Stefan Dramiński

Sheet 09

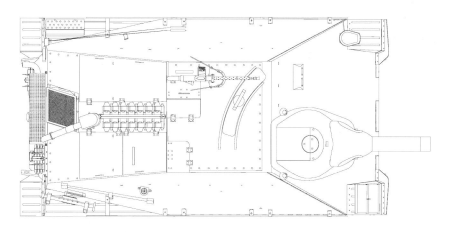

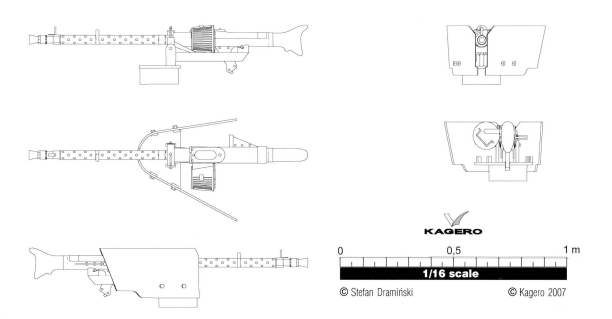

KAGERO

0   0,5   1 m

1/16 scale

© Stefan Dramiński   © Kagero 2007

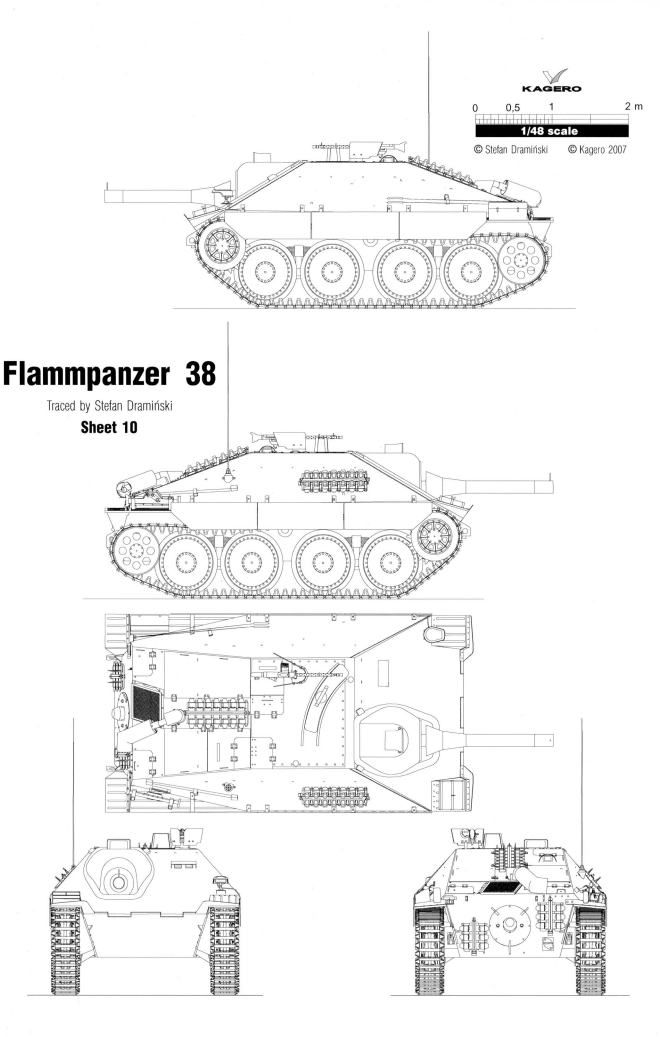

Flammpanzer 38

Traced by Stefan Dramiński

Sheet 10

0   0,5   1   2 m

1/48 scale

KAGERO

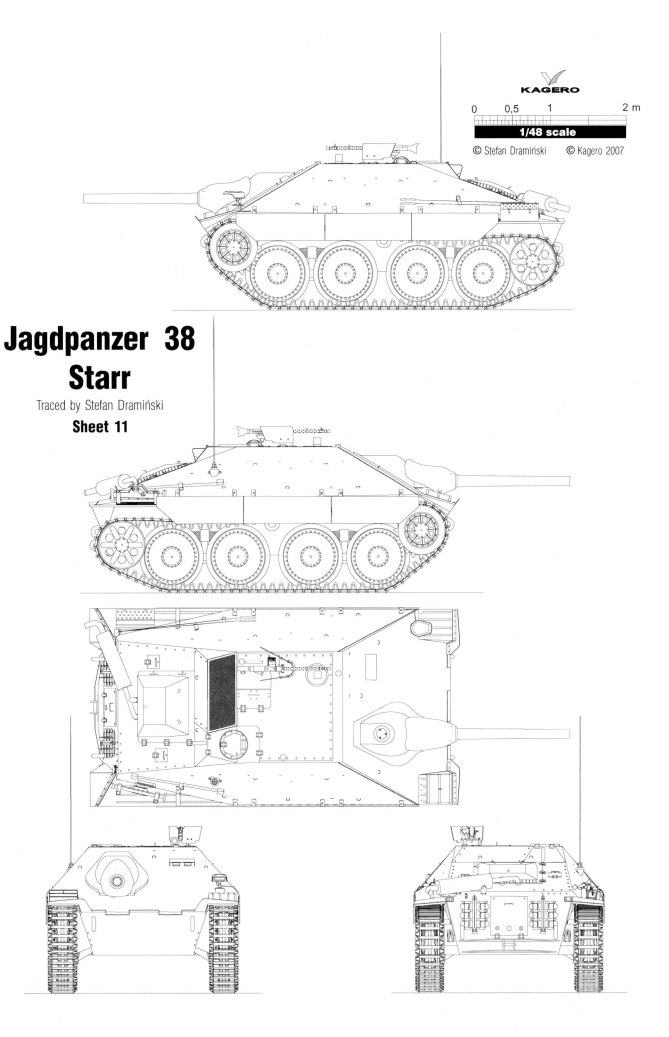

Jagdpanzer 38
Starr

Traced by Stefan Dramiński

Sheet 11

KAGERO

0   0,5   1   2 m

1/48 scale

Jagdpanzer 38
Starr

Traced by Stefan Dramiński

Sheet 12

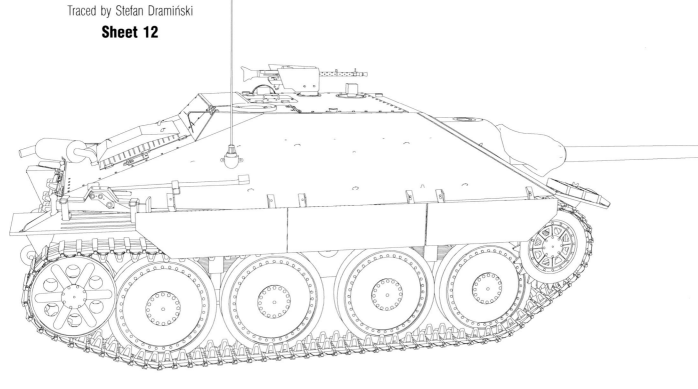

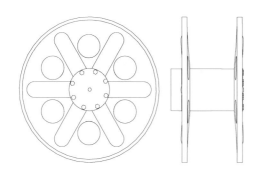

KAGERO

0   0,5   1 m

1/16 scale

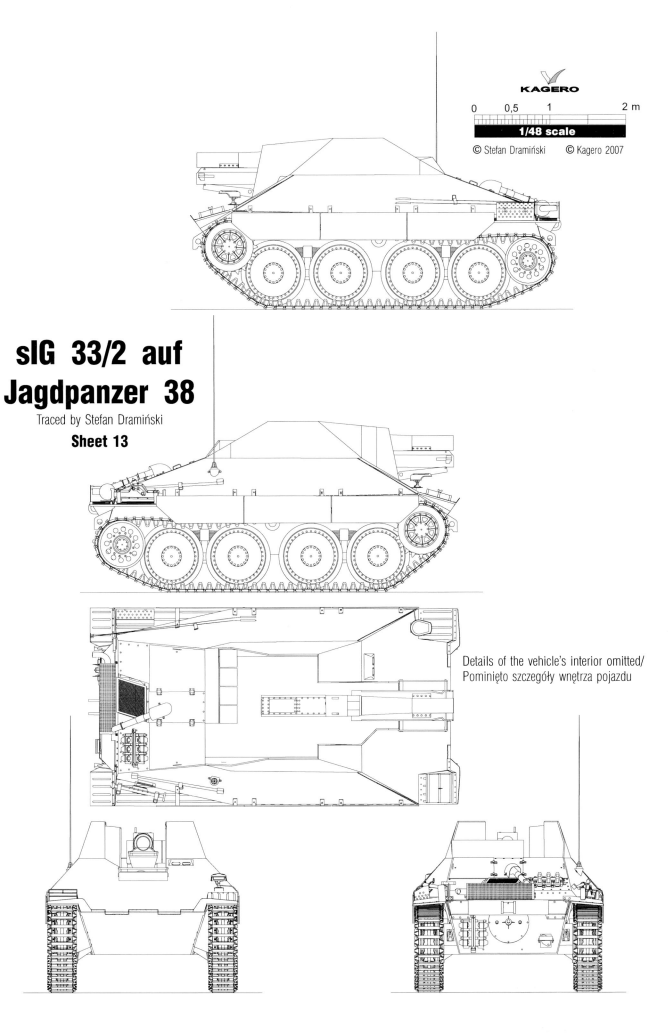

KAGERO

0   0,5   1   2 m

1/48 scale

© Stefan Dramiński   © Kagero 2007

sIG 33/2 auf
Jagdpanzer 38

Traced by Stefan Dramiński

Sheet 13

Details of the vehicle's interior omitted/
Pominięto szczegóły wnętrza pojazdu

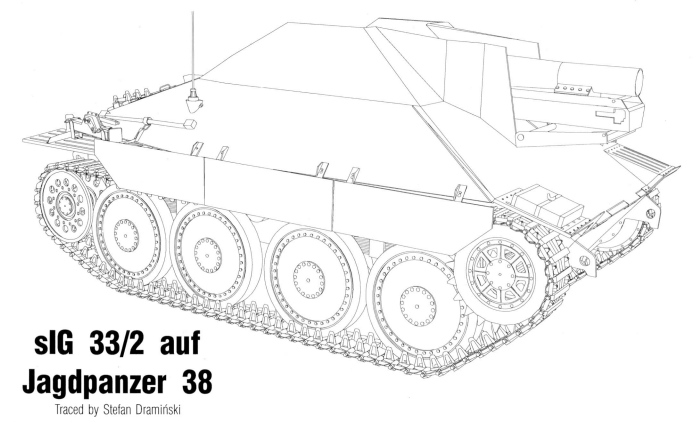

sIG 33/2 auf
Jagdpanzer 38

Traced by Stefan Dramiński

Sheet 14

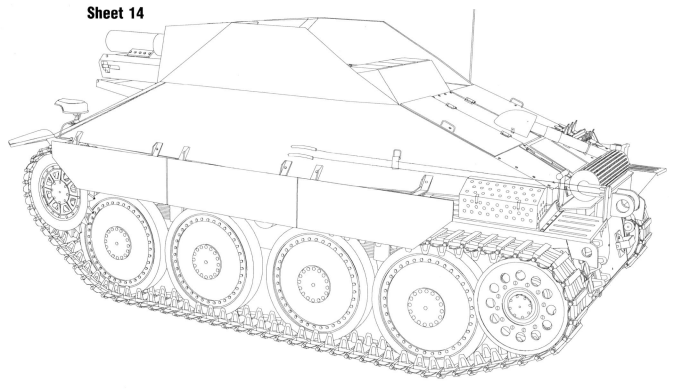

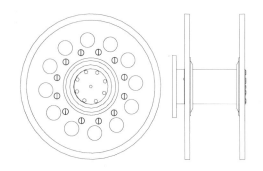

KAGERO

0   0,5   1 m

1/16 scale

© Stefan Dramiński   © Kagero 2007

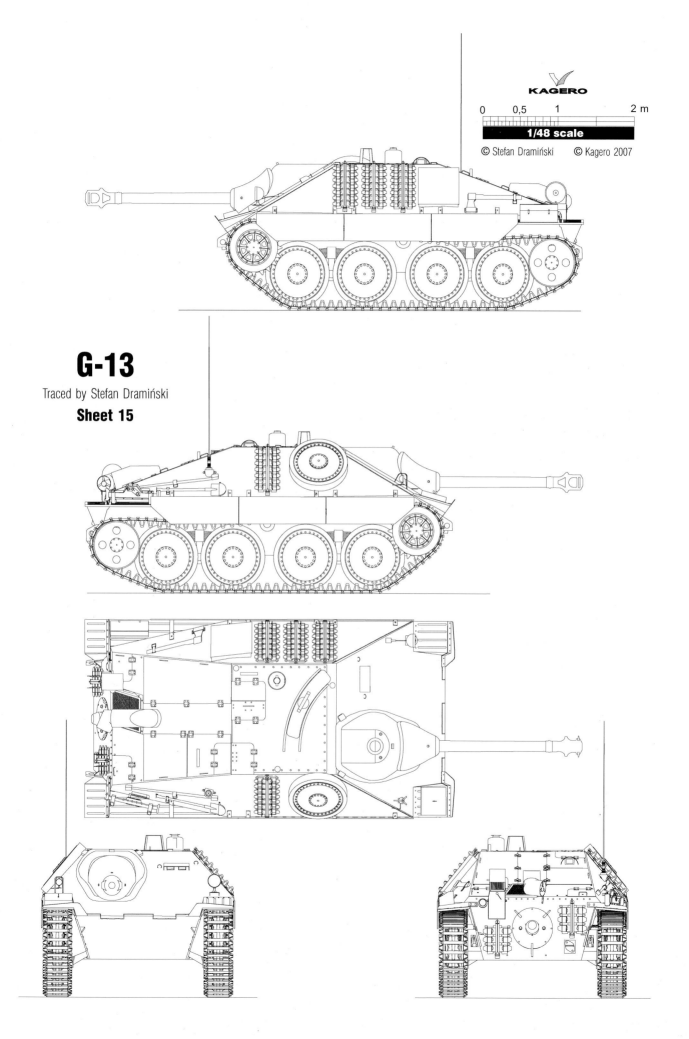

KAGERO

0   0,5   1   2 m

1/48 scale

G-13

Traced by Stefan Dramiński

Sheet 15

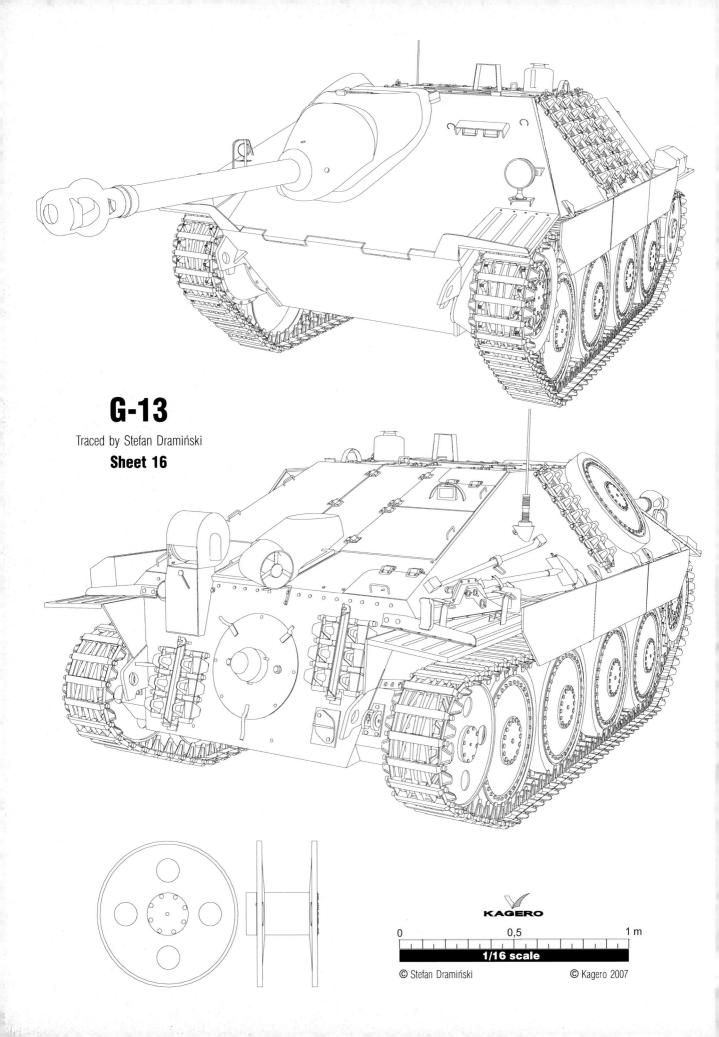

G-13

Traced by Stefan Dramiński

Sheet 16

KAGERO

0 0,5 1 m

1/16 scale

The Hetzer from Hel

Hetzer z Helu

The Hetzer self-propelled gun was abandoned in 1945 by the Germans beleaguared on the Hel peninsula on a beach between Hel and Jurata. The vehicle stood on the beach until the 80s, then it was slowly devoured by the sea. In 2005 a witness showed the place the Foundation for the Recovery of the Missing Artwork "Latebra". In early 2006 the vehicle was localized with a metal detector. During the spring and summer the equipment was being completed and the official clearances were being fixed. The first attempt of the recovery in November 2006 failed because of the rough sea. On May 26th, 2007, after several attempts the Hetzer was recovered from the sea. Sand and contamination were washed out of the interior. The equipment, ammunition, coins and other items were secured. The vehicle became a sensation; the recovery and transport were showed by all Polish TV stations. After the restoration the Hetzer will be displayed at the Motorisation Museum in Gdynia.

Działo samobieżne Hetzer zostało porzucone w 1945 roku przez okrążonych na Helu Niemców na plaży między Helem a Juratą. Sprzęt stał na plaży obok poligonu do lat osiemdziesiątych, potem powoli pogrążył się w morzu. W 2005 roku świadek wskazał to miejsce Fundacji na Rzecz Odzyskania Zaginionych Dzieł Sztuki „Latebra". Na początku 2006 roku maszyna została namierzona za pomocą detektora metali. Przez wiosnę i lato trwało kompletowanie sprzętu i załatwianie spraw urzędowych. Pierwsza próba wydobycia, w listopadzie 2006 roku nie powiodła się ze względu na zbyt wzburzone morze. 26 maja 2007 roku, po kilku próbach, Hetzer został wydobyty z morza. Z wnętrza wypłukano piach i zanieczyszczenia. Zabezpieczono wyposażenie, amunicję, monety i inne drobiazgi. Maszyna stała się sensacją; wydobycie i przewożenie pokazywały wszystkie polskie stacje telewizyjne. Po wyremontowaniu Hetzer stanie w Muzeum Motoryzacji w Gdyni.

Dominik Markiewicz)